COPYRIGHT AND LICE

PLEASE READ THIS IMPORTANT INFORMATION BEFORE PLANNING YOUR PERFORMANCE

Under the Copyrights, Designs and Patents Act (1988), it is a legal requirement for schools to comply with copyright law, and ensure they hold the correct licences for performing musicals. As experienced teachers ourselves, we understand that time restraints and lack of advice can sometimes mean this aspect of your production is not dealt with, or that the details and requirements are not fully understood. We therefore try to make the process of licensing your performances as simple as possible.

General Guidelines

You are free to use any of our material for all classroom teaching purposes and for performances within school to only pupils and staff. However, if our musicals are to be performed to an audience other than pupils and staff from your school (eg. parents or other people from the wider community) then a performance licence must be obtained directly from Edgy Productions.

Performance of Musicals

The performance of works involving drama, movement, narrative or spoken dialogue requires a title and date specific licence from the copyright holder/publisher – in this case Edgy Productions. The requirement for a licence is irrespective of admission charges. **Your PRS, PPL, CCLA or any equivalent local authority-issued licences DO NOT cover you for such performances**.

A performance licence from us will permit the holder to do the following:

- Perform a musical up to 5 times in one academic year, to a public audience, within your school.*
- Reproduce song lyrics on paper or for display on interactive whiteboards or similar screens.
- Photocopy the script and score for the cast to learn lines, and musicians to play the songs.

* **If you are performing outside of your school premises, for example in a local theatre, please contact us as further conditions apply.**
For more information, visit www.edgyproductions.com/licences

Audio and Video Recordings

If you wish to make an audio or video recording of the performance of any of our musicals, you will need an additional **recording and duplication licence** from Edgy Productions. This will also allow you to make and sell copies of your recordings if you wish to do so. We no longer request that you pay a commission to us on the money you raise from the sale of recordings.

File Sharing

You are not permitted to share any of our copyrighted material, either in printed form, on disc or in digital file format, with anyone who is not a pupil or teacher within your school or organisation. We will take immediate action should an incident of illegal file-sharing be reported or discovered.

You can, of course, phone or email us for advice – we are more than happy to discuss all your licensing needs.

Tel: 01858 288081
Email: info@edgyproductions.com

PERFORMANCE LICENCE APPLICATION FORM

For any performance of any part of **'How Christmas Came To Be'** to an audience other than staff and children (eg. if you perform to parents), a valid performance licence from Edgy Productions must be held. Please note, your PRS, MCPS, CCLI or similar local authority-issued licence does not cover you for this. **Unless you purchased a performance licence and/or a recording & duplication licence when you bought this production pack, please ensure you complete and return this form at least 28 days before your first performance:**

- by post – Edgy Productions, 8 Roman Way, Market Harborough, Leicestershire LE16 7PQ
- by FAX – 0845 833 33 49
- by email – info@edgyproductions.com

The performance licence will permit the holder to do the following:
- Perform a musical up to 5 times in one academic year, to a public audience, within your school.*
- Reproduce song lyrics on paper or for display on interactive whiteboards or similar screens.
- Photocopy the script and score for the cast to learn lines, and musicians to play the songs.

Contact name: ....

Name of school / organisation: ....

Address: ....

.... **Postcode:** ....

Tel: .... **email:** ....

Number of performances: ...... **Performances Dates: from** .... **to** ....

By ticking, select one of the performance licence options below:

Standard Performance Licence
(**no** admission charged and **no** tickets sold) ☐ **£30.00** *(including VAT)*

or

Performance Licence with charges
(admission **is** charged and/or tickets **are** sold) ☐ **£36.00** *(including VAT)*

☐ * Tick if you are performing outside your school premises, for example in a local theatre, as further conditions apply – see www.edgyproductions.com/licences

---

If you are recording any performance, and/or selling copies of the recording, you will *also* need a recording and duplication licence.

Recording and Duplication Licence ☐ **£30.00** *(including VAT)*

By ticking, select one of the payment options below:

☐ **I enclose a cheque for £.......... made payable to Edgy Productions Ltd**

☐ **Please send me an invoice for £..........** *(payment terms 30 days)*

**Writers rely on payments from public performances for their livelihoods.
Please ensure they receive their dues.**

PLOT SUMMARY

The audience is warmly welcomed by our five hosts, each of them either a famous Christmas character, or someone from a period in history which had an influence on our modern-day Christmas. Through them, and the scenes and songs they introduce, we get a fascinating and thoroughly entertaining insight into how Christmas developed through the ages into the festival we know and love today. *(song – A Time To Celebrate)*

Firstly, we are taken back to ancient Rome during the festival of 'Saturnalia', when the winter solstice was celebrated in quite an unusual way. An old grandfather, Senilius, is bewildered by the bizarre antics of his family who enthusiastically embrace the festival's practice of social-role reversal! This could explain why the household slave, Lavatoria, is wearing expensive clothes and is refusing to do as she's told! *(song – Saturnalia)*

Next, we join the Norsemen of northern Europe during their festival of Yule. As Olaf prepares to light the Yule log and tap open his barrels of home-brewed ale, can he escape the advances of his wife, Astrid, who is stalking him round their homestead with a sprig of mistletoe? *(song – Banish The Winter Blues)*

We then learn how, once Christianity became widespread in the 4th century, the Festival of the Nativity was introduced and December 25th became the official date to celebrate the birth of Jesus. While the feasting, the giving of gifts and other customs carried on from the existing winter festivals, the reason for doing these things had now changed forever – Christmas had arrived! As a Nativity tableau is presented, the audience is entertained with a rousing bit of gospel music! *(song – Hallelujah!)*

After hearing how things developed through the middle ages and Tudor times, the mid-17th century is our next stop, as we encounter the Puritan ban on all things Christmassy! As three soldiers try to enforce this ban by confiscating food, drink and presents from festive revellers, not all goes according to plan and one lucky individual finds a way to keep the party going! *(song – No More Christmas)*

In so many ways the Victorian age saw Christmas becoming more like the festival we recognise today. In our next scene, as an excited Prince Albert brings home the first Christmas tree, Queen Victoria is definitely 'not amused' at having to sweep up pine needles from the palace floor! *(song – The Victorians)*

Our final destination is the North Pole, where we meet the biggest icon of our modern Christmas. After learning how the early persona of Santa Claus developed over the centuries, we meet him right in the middle of an image crisis! With some expert professional help, this crisis is averted and he settles on a look (and a catchphrase) that will forever capture the imagination of children everywhere! *(song – Ho! Ho! Ho!)*

And now, with Santa's use of the internet allowing children to track his progress around the globe on Christmas Eve, our journey is brought bang up to date. As our hosts wish us well for the festive season, we are reminded that one message above any other should be kept at the heart of Christmas – goodwill to one and all!
(song – Roll On Christmas Day)

CHARACTERS

For larger schools, extra speaking characters can be added to scenes and the existing lines shared out between them, or new lines created. For smaller schools, as most characters only appear in one scene, multiple parts (including ensemble characters) can be played by a single actor.

---

37 speaking parts in order of appearance

Hosts:
Rudolph – a red-nosed reindeer
Gabriel – a well-known angel
Charles Dickens – a prominent Victorian
Erika Winterbörn – a pagan Norsewoman
Festivius Maximus – a Roman citizen

Celebrating the Roman festival of Saturnalia:
Senilius – a doddery grandfather
Tipsius – his merry son, husband to...
Violentia – a mother and part-time female gladiator
Bratius & Moodica – their son and daughter
Lavatoria – a slave

Celebrating the festival of Yule:
Olaf – a Norseman
Astrid – his mistletoe-carrying wife
3 Cows – aware of their impending doom

The nativity tableau:
Mary
Joseph
A Donkey
An Angel
A Shepherd
A Wise Man

Suffering a Puritan Christmas:
3 Soldiers – on a mission to stop celebrations
4 Revellers – on a mission to celebrate

Enjoying a Victorian Christmas:
Prince Albert – proud of his tree
3 Children – excited by his tree
Queen Victoria – 'not amused' by his tree

Making preparations at the North Pole:
Santa – having an image crisis
Mrs Santa – his supportive wife
Wok Ho – fashion advisor to the stars

(Ensemble characters for featured songs and scenes)

Poor and wealthy Romans
Female Gladiators
Norsemen and women
Traditional Nativity characters
Puritans and Revellers
Victorians
A team of Reindeer
Santa's Elves

For a character line-count & costume suggestions see p29

If using our digital backdrops, select 'backdrop 1'

Scene 1

*(As the **intro music** plays **(track 9)** the whole cast enters. All sit on and around the main stage. The five 'hosts', each a character associated with Christmas or winter festivals through the ages, stand centre-stage to address the audience. Their lines throughout can be read – they have quite a few!)*

All SEASON'S GREETINGS, ONE AND ALL!

Rudolph Well, here we are at the end of a very long term, but still with a few more days left at school! *(The whole cast groans!)*

Gabriel And seeing as school's not quite finished yet, we thought we'd cram in a bit more learning while we have the chance! *(The whole cast groans again!)* Oh come on, don't be like that! Learning can be fun, especially when the thing you're learning about is.....Christmas!

Charles Dickens Yes, Christmas! Everyone's favourite time of year! A decorated tree, turkey, crackers, mince pies and watching Great Granny dancing to an old festive pop song after one too many sherries!

Erika Winterbörn But it hasn't always been like that, which is why we're here to take you on an entertaining, musical journey through history, to show you how the Christmas we know and love came to be!

Festivius Maximus Now, apart from a couple of characters standing here, you may be looking at the five of us and wondering what on earth we have to do with Christmas! Well, let us introduce ourselves, then all will become clear. My name is Festivius Maximus, a Roman citizen. In a moment you'll find out how our ancient customs and festivals were an early influence on the modern Christmas.

Erika W. And I'm Erika Winterbörn, a pagan Norsewoman from northern Europe. Our people also held celebrations in the bleak mid-winter, which included strange customs that are still a part of Christmas today! We'll be sharing some of these with you later.

Gabriel I'm Gabriel, the famous angel, and I played an important part in the story that really started the ball rolling and which gave Christmas its name. More about that in a while.

Charles D. And I'm Charles Dickens, one of the best-known writers from the 19th century. You're going to learn how the Victorians (and my stories) started shaping Christmas into the festival we recognise nowadays.

Rudolph Well, my antlers and red nose are a dead give-away, aren't they! I'm Rudolph, a friend and helper to someone who has become the most recognisable character in our modern celebrations. You'll be hearing about his rise to Christmas super-stardom in a bit!

Gabriel But before all that, we promised you some entertainment and music, so let's have a song! *(to the cast)* Okay you lot, on your feet!

Song A Time To Celebrate

(tracks 1 & 10, lyrics p19)

(The whole cast)

(All then sit to the side and in front of the stage, apart from the five hosts who stand centrally.)

Festivius M. Right, let's crack on! First we're going to travel back to my era, ancient Rome. During the week before the winter solstice, the shortest day of our calendar year, around December 25th, we Romans celebrated the festival of Saturnalia. Hmmm, December 25th? Does that date sound familiar?

Erika W. Saturnalia was a whole week of feasting and drinking, all done in honour of Saturn, the Roman god of Agriculture.

Gabriel Because it was a time for having fun, for exchanging gifts and also because of when it was celebrated, Saturnalia was a big influence on the development of Christmas as we know it.

Charles D. But what really made Saturnalia enjoyable was the tradition of 'social role-reversal'. For example, slaves would become masters of a household and the masters would become slaves for a whole week!

Rudolph Women would take part in gladiator fights and wealthy citizens would dress in rags and give away lots of money to the poor! Everything went kind of topsy-turvy in ancient Rome during Saturnalia and we reckon it might have looked a little something like this..........

If using our digital backdrops, select 'backdrop 2'

*(To the sound of a **harp (track 11)** the five hosts exit. Leaning on a walking stick, a doddery Roman grandfather, Senilius, enters and sits on a stool centre stage. He wears a traditional toga. His son, Tipsius, excitedly enters, dressed in rags and carrying a goblet.)*

Tipsius Happy Saturnalia, Father!

Senilius *(straining to hear)* Speak up Tipsius. You know I'm deaf.

Tipsius *(loudly)* I said happy Saturnalia! You should try this wine by the way, it's excellent. I'm on my third goblet already! Well, when in Rome!

Senilius Saturnalia? What are you talking about?

Tipsius It's our festival to celebrate the solstice, remember? We eat, drink and exchange gifts. Ooh, that reminds me....*(shouting)* Bratius! Moodica!

(Bratius and Moodica enter. They are also dressed in rags. Moodica carries a parcel.)

Tipsius Ah, children, there you are! Bratius, give your grandfather his gift.

Bratius *(handing Senilius the parcel and speaking loudly)* Happy Saturnalia, Grandfather. This is from all of us.

(Senilius unwraps the gift, which is an ear-trumpet. He looks at it with confusion.)

Moodica *(speaking loudly)* It's an ear-trumpet, Grandfather. Hold it to your ear and you'll be able to hear everyone without them having to shout!

Senilius Oh, thank you children. *(holding it to his ear)* Well, say something then.

Tipsius, Bratius & Moodica HAPPY SATURNALIA!

Senilius *(jumping in shock!)* Alright, alright! No need to yell at me! Now tell me, why are you three dressed in rags?

(Senilius keeps the ear trumpet to his ear for the whole of the following dialogue.)

Bratius Because it's Saturnalia, when everything gets turned upside down!

Moodica We're a wealthy family, so we dress like we're poor. It's great fun!

Senilius Well, it doesn't sound like fun to me. Those rags must be awfully itchy. And is your mother joining in too? Where is she?

(Dressed in armour, their mother, Violentia, enters, jabbing at the air with a sword.)

Violentia Take that! And that! And that! Oh, I tell you what, I can't wait for the big fight this afternoon! I'm drawn against that busy-body, Gossipa! I've been waiting ages for the chance to give her what for! Take that!

Tipsius And, Violentia my dear, we'll all be at the Colosseum to cheer you on!

Senilius Hang on! Why on earth are women taking part in gladiator fights?

T, B, M & V BECAUSE IT'S SATURNALIA!

Senilius Saturnalia – pfff! Where's our slave by the way? I need a cushion for this stool. Lavatoria! LAVATORIA! COME HERE NOW!

(Lavatoria enters, dressed in fine robes and jewellery.)

Lavatoria Don't shout at me, Senilius! It's about time you learned your place! And why is my lunch not ready? I've been waiting an hour!

Senilius Impudent girl! Have you taken leave of your senses?! And why are you dressed up in those fine clothes? You're a slave!

Violentia Ahem, Senilius, you can't talk to Lavatoria like that. She is *not* your slave, you're *hers*! You should really get her lunch if she's asked you.

Senilius What?! Don't be ridiculous! Me, a slave? To her? Why?

T, B, M, V & L BECAUSE IT'S SATURNALIA!

(The five crowd behind the stool, loudly explaining different aspects of Saturnalia to the confused Senilius. He stands up and walks to the front of the stage, the five following behind and still talking loudly. He then removes the ear-trumpet from his ear and we immediately can't hear his family's voices, though they carry on mouthing words as if they're still talking to him.)

Senilius *(to the audience)* Ah, peace and quiet. You know, I think I prefer being deaf than having to listen to all that nonsense, *(throwing down the ear trumpet)* so I won't be needing this thing! And as for Saturnalia....well, I guess there are some things that I'm just too old to understand!

*(As the **intro music** plays **(track 12)**, the family gathers at the front of the stage for the next song. They are joined by more female gladiators, poor Romans and wealthy Romans. Fade the music when all are ready to sing.)*

Song Saturnalia *(tracks 2 & 13, lyrics p20)*

(The Roman family, supported by the whole cast)

*(As the **intro music** then plays **(track 14)**, all sit and the stage is prepared for the next scene. When ready, the five hosts return and stand centrally.)*

If using our digital backdrops, select 'backdrop 1'

Scene 2

Festivius M. How are we enjoying it so far? You see, learning can be fun! So, let's move things along here, shall we? Erika, over to you.

Erika W. Thanks Festivius. Well, in the early centuries AD, we pagans from northern Europe also celebrated the winter solstice. Like the Romans, we feasted and drank a lot to mark the start of the days getting longer. We called this celebration 'Yule', a word which might sound familiar to you.

Gabriel In Scandinavia, they would cut a huge Yule log to burn throughout the celebrations, which would last for twelve days. Hmm, twelve days of Yule and a log – a couple more things you might recognise!

Charles D. The cattle were slaughtered so they wouldn't need feeding throughout the remaining colder months. All this fresh meat provided plenty to feast upon during Yule and for the rest of the winter. Also, with barrels of fermented ale ready to crack open, Yule really was a time for merriment, with the toast 'Skål!' being shouted at every opportunity!

Rudolph Evergreen leaves were used to decorate homes, to represent long life and good fortune. One particular plant, mistletoe, was hung up in dedication to Frigga, the Norse goddess of love. We all know what goes on under mistletoe these days, and it was the same back then.

Erika W. We reckon it might have looked a little something like this.........

If using our digital backdrops, select 'backdrop 3'

*(To the sound of a **harp (track 15)** the five hosts exit. Three cows enter – **see staging suggestions/costumes** – and stand to one side of the stage. Olaf enters, carrying a large log which he places on top of a small pile of twigs centre-stage. The cows watch him.)*

Olaf There, that should easily burn for twelve days. Right, let's get it lit!

(Just as he bends down, off-stage we hear the raucous voice of his wife, Astrid!)

Astrid   Olaf! Oh, Olaf! Where are you? I have a surprise for you!

Olaf   *(jumping up)* Oh no! My wife, Astrid! I bet I know what she's after! I need to hide, quickly!

(He hides behind the cows. Astrid enters, scouring the stage, holding up a sprig of mistletoe!)

Astrid   Olaf! Come out, come out, wherever you are! I've got mistletoe! Olaf! OLAF!

(Astrid exits in search of her husband. Olaf then emerges from behind the cows.)

Olaf   Phew! That was a close call! Right, I'd better go and get those barrels of ale tapped. Solstice celebrations are not the same without Olaf's famous home brew!

(He exits in the opposite direction to Astrid. She returns, still holding up the mistletoe, but looking a bit more annoyed.)

Astrid   Olaf! OLAF! *(to the audience)* A kiss once a year is hardly asking too much, is it? Oh, where is the wretched man. OLAF!

(She exits in the opposite direction to Olaf. The cows watch her go and hang their heads.)

Cow 1   Did you catch all that? Him bringing in a log and cracking open his home brew, and her pacing around with mistletoe? *(gulping nervously)* It can mean only one thing!

Cow 2   Yule is here! There'll be lots of drinking and lots of.....feasting. And what will they be feasting on? Us!

Cow 3   Well my friends, it's been a pleasure growing fat with you these past months, but it appears our numbers are finally up. Happy Yule!

*(As some famous **mournful music** plays **(track 16)** the cows shake hands with each other and, if you think it appropriate, each pretends to light up a large cigar – the last act of a condemned cow! As the music fades, Olaf then enters with a barrel which he places by the fire.)*

Olaf   There, that's the ale sorted! Right, let's think about the meat.

(He approaches the cows, takes hold of the ropes round their necks and leads them to the front of the stage. Astrid, unseen by Olaf tiptoes on with the mistletoe held up. She then grabs him from behind and he drops the cows' ropes!)

Astrid   Gotcha! Oh, Olaf, my big, bearded beauty! Give us a kiss!

(As Astrid tries to kiss Olaf, he keeps her at arm's length and a comical struggle follows. During this, the cows nudge each other and nimbly tiptoe off stage, making their escape! Astrid finally manages to plant a kiss on Olaf's cheek then releases him! Olaf grimaces and wipes his cheek!)

Olaf   Astrid! Please! We have Yule celebrations to prepare for. If you really want to put your energy into something, you can help with the cows.

(Both turn to where the cows should be!)

Olaf   Where have they gone?! Oh no! We've got no meat for our feast! That's your fault, Astrid! What are we going to do now?

Astrid   *(holding up the mistletoe)* Oh, I'm sure we can think of something!

*(As the **intro music** plays **(track 17)**, Olaf bolts off stage with Astrid in hot pursuit! Other Norsemen and women, plus the cows, enter and stand centre-stage. Olaf and Astrid then return, holding hands. Fade the music when ready to sing the next song.)*

Song # Banish The Winter Blues

(tracks 3 & 18, lyrics p21)

(The Norse people, supported by the whole cast)

*(As the **intro music** then plays **(track 19)**, all sit and the stage is prepared for the next scene. When ready, the five hosts return and stand centrally.)*

If using our digital backdrops, select 'backdrop 1'

Scene 3

Erika W.   So, we're learning that the old festivals had a big influence on modern celebrations, with lots of features we still see today. I must say, mistletoe is definitely one of my favourites!

Gabriel   But things really took a turn when the life and teachings of Jesus Christ became important to the Romans. In the 4th century AD, under the emperor Constantine, Christianity became the main religion of the Roman Empire.

Charles D.   Now, the bible told of the people, places and events surrounding the birth of Jesus, but there was no date mentioned and so no holiday or festival could be organised to celebrate it.

Festivius M.   But then in the middle of the 4th century, Pope Julius 1st declared that Jesus' birth should be celebrated on December 25th, when the festival of Saturnalia was happening. In that way, the Romans could still have their merry time during the winter solstice, but the reasons for celebration would now be different.

Rudolph   And so the 'Festival of the Nativity' was introduced. The story of the birth of God's son in a stable in Bethlehem would now and forever be at the heart of winter festivities. Although the actual word wouldn't be used until the 11th century, 'Christmas' had truly arrived!

Gabriel   And it's a story we love to tell again and again, especially at school. The familiar characters of Mary, Joseph, a donkey, shepherds, wise men and of course me, the angel Gabriel, all come together to help us understand why we really celebrate Christmas. And, of course, it looks a little something like this.........

(If using our digital backdrops, select 'backdrop 4')

*(To the **harp** (track 20) the other hosts exit - Gabriel remains. The Nativity characters enter and form a traditional tableau, with Gabriel standing behind Mary and the manger.)*

Mary   God chose me to have His baby. Although I was frightened, I trusted in Him and was honoured to be part of His plan.

Joseph   And my support of Mary also shows how we all trust in God's will and how we are thankful for the gift He gave to the world.

Angel   Our presence throughout the Nativity story reminds us that, at Christmas, Heaven and Earth are as one, and our joyful praises show that the birth of Jesus was a cause for wonderful celebration.

Donkey   The lowly stable where Jesus was born reminds us that He would be a peaceful man and that His kingdom would be unlike any other.

Shepherd   We were the first visitors to kneel at the manger where Jesus lay. We humble shepherds symbolise the love that He would show to all people, whether rich or poor.

Wise Man   And we three wise men brought gifts for Jesus, which showed how Christmas would become a time for giving and sharing. The gold, frankincense and myrrh we gave Him symbolised His greatness, His holiness and the sacrifice He would eventually make.

Gabriel   This scene here on stage was to become the true picture of Christmas. It would inspire great art and fabulous music which we still see and hear to this day. So everyone, on your feet once more as we celebrate what Christmas is really all about!

Song # Hallelujah! *(tracks 4 & 21, lyrics p22)*

(The Nativity characters, supported by the whole cast)

*(As the **intro music** then plays (track 22), all sit and the stage is cleared ready for the next scene. When ready, the five hosts return and stand centrally.)*

(If using our digital backdrops, select 'backdrop 1')

Scene 4

Gabriel   How uplifting! I tell you what, it's starting to feel a lot like Christmas!

Rudolph   So, by the 8th century, festivities were happening throughout the Christian world. The birth of Jesus was a good excuse for everyone to cut loose for a few days each winter and have a really good time!

Festivius M.   During the middle ages things got really raucous, with Mardis Gras-type celebrations occurring. A 'Lord of Misrule' would be crowned – a beggar whose job it was to terrorize wealthier people with mischief if they didn't hand over their best food and drink when it was demanded!

Charles D. Then, in the courts of the Tudor and Stuart monarchs, the feasting became very extravagant, with a menu of goose, swan, peacock and meat-filled mince pies shaped like a crib. In 1519 the first turkey was introduced to Britain, although it would be many years before it became a traditional Christmas dish.

Erika W. But to some it seemed that we had lost sight of what Christmas should be about. With the English civil war in the mid-17th century, when Oliver Cromwell came to power, things certainly changed!

Gabriel Under Cromwell and the Puritans, who had very strict religious rules, Christmas would no longer be a holiday or a time for fun. Soldiers patrolled the streets and would arrest anyone who looked like they were partying!

Rudolph They would even confiscate food and drink that they suspected was being prepared in celebration of Christmas! Alcohol was banned, as was the decorating of homes and, unless it fell on a Sunday, December 25th was a day for working and business as usual.

Festivius M. Puritans believed that only hard work and avoiding pleasurable pastimes would gain you a place in heaven. So, for a while at least, it was curtains for Christmas, even though most people were not happy about it. We reckon it might have looked a little something like this......

If using our digital backdrops, select 'backdrop 5'

*(To the sound of a **harp (track 23)** the five hosts exit. Three Cromwellian soldiers enter carrying pikes (spears) and stand centre-stage.)*

Soldier 1 So, this is fun...not! I used to really enjoy Christmas!

Soldier 2 Shhh! You can't talk like that anymore! We've got a job to do!

Soldier 3 That's right. Now, are we clear what our orders are? We have to stop anyone who looks like they might be celebrating Christmas and seize any food, drink or parcels they're carrying.

Soldier 1 Really? Why?

Soldier 2 To save their souls of course, so they'll go to heaven. Look, here comes a suspicious-looking character.

(A reveller enters carrying a parcel.)

Reveller 1 *(singing)* We wish you a merry Christmas, we wish you a merry Christmas, we wish you a merry Chri....*(seeing the soldiers)*...oh! Errr. Yes, I'm just on my way to...to...to church. Yes, to church!

Soldier 2 With a parcel? You must think we were born yesterday! C'mon, hand it over.

Reveller 1 *(angrily handing over the parcel)* Oh take it then, you joyless, mean-spirited so and so.

(Soldier 2 puts the parcel on the floor and shouts after the exiting reveller.)

Soldier 2   Oi! Less of the attitude, or we'll be locking you up!

Soldier 1   Well, that person did have a point. This all does seem pretty mean!

Soldier 3   Enough of that talk! It sounds like you want to go back to the old ways.

Soldier 1   You mean when Christmas was a happy, fun time? *(sarcastically)* Why would I possibly want to do that?

(Two more revellers enter carrying shopping baskets of food. They see the soldiers and freeze!)

Soldier 3   'Ello, 'ello, 'ello! What's all this then? Planning a get-together are we?

Reveller 2   You mean all this stuff? No, no, no! It's just our normal weekly shop.

Reveller 3   We have teenagers at home, and you know how they can eat! This is for them! It's got nothing whatsoever to do with a Christmas party!

Soldier 3   Yeah, yeah. Just leave it all down here and be on your way. Scram!

(They drop their shopping and exit.)

Soldier 1   Oh, come on! Was that really necessary? Those poor people!

Soldier 2   I'm beginning to wonder whether your heart is really in this job! We are on a mission here and that means coming down hard on those who break the rules!

(A rather 'merry' reveller enters, drinking from a tankard and staggering slightly!)

Reveller 4   *(singing)* We wish you a merry Christmas, we wish you a merry Chri.... *(seeing the soldiers)* Ah, hello my fine fellows! Season's greetings to you!

Soldier 3   Someone doesn't seem to understand the rules! I'll just relieve you of that and then a night in jail should help. Come on!

(Soldier 3 takes the tankard and puts it down, then with Soldier 2 escorts the reveller off-stage. Soldier 1 is left alone! He checks to see the others have gone, then gathers up all the items.)

Soldier 1   Well, waste not want not, eh! *(exiting whilst singing)* We wish you a merry Christmas, we wish you a merry Christmas.........!

*(As the **intro music** then plays **(track 24)**, the soldiers and revellers return. They are joined by other Puritans, soldiers and revellers. Fade the music when ready to sing the next song.)*

Song # No More Christmas

(tracks 5 & 25, lyrics p23)

(Soldiers, Revellers and Puritans, supported by the whole cast)

*(As the **intro music** then plays **(track 26)**, all sit and the stage is prepared for the next scene. When ready, the five hosts return and stand centrally.)*

Scene 5

If using our digital backdrops, select 'backdrop 1'

Festivius M. That was a pretty awful way to spend Christmas, wasn't it? But thankfully, for those who missed the good times, they would return with the 'Restoration', when in 1660 Charles the 2nd became king.

Rudolph And he was a king who liked to party, so Christmas again became a public holiday and a time to celebrate!

Erika W. But it was during the Victorian age that it started to become more like the Christmas we recognise today. Mr Dickens, over to you....

Charles D. During the 19th century, people became more aware of the need for kindness and goodwill to those who were struggling. My stories, such as Oliver Twist, made everyone think about caring for and protecting children. Then, with my novel A Christmas Carol, I drew attention to how the poor needed help and support, especially at Christmas time.

Gabriel The image of a family together, sharing food, presents and games, and with the children at the centre of things, really captured the nation's imagination during Victorian times.

Rudolph And it saw the introduction of many of the features we see in our Christmas celebrations today; crackers, Christmas cards, carol singers, fruit-filled mince pies, and the all-important turkey dinner – but only for wealthier families.

Charles D. And when Queen Victoria married Prince Albert, he introduced something from Germany that has stayed with us ever since – the Christmas tree! We reckon it might have looked a little something like this......

If using our digital backdrops, select 'backdrop 6'

*(To the sound of a **harp (track 27)** the five hosts exit. Prince Albert excitedly enters, carrying an undecorated Christmas tree – this should be a green artificial one on a stand. He places it centre stage, then fetches a box of decorations.)*

Albert Zer! Doesn't zat look fantastic! Children! Come und zee vat I haf here!

(Three children enter and look at the tree.)

Child 1 But what is it, Papa?

Albert It ist ein Christmas tree! Ve haf zem in Germany und zey make zee house festive und jolly!

Child 2 But it doesn't look festive and jolly, Papa. It's a bit plain!

Albert *(pointing to the box)* Vich is vy I haf lots of pretty zings ve can put on it!

(The children excitedly rummage through the box!)

Child 3 And do we just put all these on the tree wherever we like?

Albert   Of course! *(picking up the angel decoration)* But not zis angel. Ve put zis on ze top of ze tree ven ve haf finished!

(They quickly dress the tree with baubles and tinsel! The children then squabble over the angel!)

Albert   Children! Do not squabble. Ve vill put ze angel on ze tree together.

(They hold the angel and place it on the tree together, then stand back to admire it.)

Child 1   Oh Papa, it's beautiful!

Child 2   It really does make our palace feel cosy and warm for Christmas!

Child 3   I think Mama is going to love it too!

(We hear Victoria's voice from off-stage.)

Victoria   Albert! Albert! Where are you?

Albert   In here, mein pumpernickel! Kom und see vat ve haf done!

(Victoria enters carrying a dustpan and brush. She does not look happy!)

Victoria   Albert! There are green spiky things all over the floor, from the front door through every room in the palace? It has taken me ages to sweep them up! What have you been doing?!

Albert   Ah, mein strudel! Zey are pine needles from our beautiful new Christmas tree! Tell me, vat do you think?

Victoria   *(mimicking him)* 'Vat' do I think? I'll tell you 'vat' I think. The rest of the royal family will be here for Christmas dinner in ten minutes and I'm clearing up your mess! Albert....we are not amused!

*(As the **intro music** then plays **(track 28)**, the family are joined by more Victorians. Fade the music when ready to sing the next song.)*

Song **The Victorians** (tracks 6 & 29, lyrics p24)

(The Victorians, supported by the whole cast)

*(As the **intro music** then plays **(track 30)**, all sit and the stage is prepared for the next scene. When ready, the five hosts return and stand centrally.)*

If using our digital backdrops, select 'backdrop 1'

Scene 6

Charles D.   The Victorian age – a time of great changes in many ways. So, finally it's time to think about someone who is the very image of the modern-day Christmas. Rudolph, over to you.

Rudolph   Thank you Charles. Well, what can I say about my boss? Father Christmas, Santa Claus, Papa Noël, Saint Nick….he's had lots of names over the centuries.

Festivius M.   Over the centuries? You mean he's that old?!

Rudolph   Indeed he is! Saint Nicholas was a 4th century bishop from Turkey who was known for giving gifts to the poor. He would travel from town to town, helping those in need.

Erica W.   Rather than embarrassing a poor family by bringing gifts to their door, one story tells of him dropping coins down their chimney. These coins landed in the daughter's stockings that were hanging by the fire to dry.

Gabriel.   As the years passed and Christmas became a popular festival, it was told that children's presents would be delivered by Father Christmas. He would travel round the world on Christmas Eve, coming down the chimneys of houses to leave gifts in stockings.

Festivius M.   In 1823, a poem called 'Twas The Night Before Christmas' by Clement Clarke Moore, with a famous illustration by Thomas Nast, really set in stone Santa's image as a jolly, plump man spreading festive happiness!

Rudolph   And since then, through many stories, songs, films and TV adverts by companies such as Coca-Cola, he is now the face of our modern Christmas. And just to give you a chuckle, we reckon his image today may have come about like this…..

If using our digital backdrops, select 'backdrop 7'

*(To the sound of a **harp (track 31)** the five hosts exit. A bearded Santa, dressed only in underpants and vest, sits in a rocking-chair centre stage. He looks fed up! Mrs Santa enters and hands him a cup of tea.)*

Mrs Santa   There you are, dear, drink that. Now tell me, what's the matter?

Santa   I'm having an image crisis! For centuries now I've just been seen as a kind old man in green bishop's robes. That's okay, but times have moved on and I need to, well, jazz things up a bit.

Mrs Santa   I thought that was the problem, which is why I've invited someone along to help. *(beckoning off-stage)* Okay, he'll see you now.

*(As the **fashion theme tune** plays **(track 32)**, the flamboyant fashion stylist, Wok Ho, makes a big entrance. A parody of Gok Wan, he should adopt his famous mannerisms!)*

Wok Ho   I am Wok Ho, stylist to the stars, here to make you look fab…u…lous!

Mrs Santa   Isn't it exciting, dear? Mr Ho is going to give you a makeover!

Santa   A makeover! Well thank you! That's exactly what I need!

Wok Ho   Right, let's get started! So, for a long time now you've been wearing green, is that right? Well, green is so last year, which is why we're going to go for…..yellow! *(He clicks his fingers.)*

(An elf enters with a yellow outfit on a hanger. Santa stands and Wok Ho holds it up against him.)

Wok Ho   *(to Mrs Santa)* What do think, girlfriend?

Mrs Santa   Hmmm. I'm not sure, Mr Ho. Won't he look like a daffodil in that?

Wok Ho   Okay, well, not everyone can carry off yellow. How about....*(clicking)*

(Another elf enters carrying a pink outfit on a hanger. Wok Ho holds it up against Santa.)

Santa   Really? I mean, I'm up for a radical change of image....but pink?!

Wok Ho   I guess it is a bold step. So, let's think....what colour really says 'jolly'? Something that reflects those rosy cheeks perhaps. I wonder....*(clicking)*

(A third elf enters carrying a red outfit on a hanger. Wok Ho holds it up against Santa.)

Mrs Santa   That's it! Perfect! Oh my dear, how handsome you'll look! Put it on!

(Santa puts the suit on.)

Wok Ho   We'll just accessorize it with this belt...*(putting the belt round Santa's waist)*....and there we are! Don't you look the part!

(Everyone gasps in admiration! The reindeer enter with tinsel on their antlers.)

Wok Ho   And look, we've added a bit of sparkle to your team of reindeer too! Now you're ready to hit the skies in style. You look fab...u...lous!

(Santa proudly parades around to the applause of all. He then stops....)

Santa   But wait, there's something missing. I look the part, that's for sure, but, I don't know, I need something else....a catchphrase! That's it, I need a catchphrase! Any suggestions, Mr Ho?

(Wok Ho is staring at Santa, so transfixed at his transformation that he doesn't hear him.)

Mrs Santa   Mr Ho? A catchphrase for Santa? What do you think? Mr Ho? Mr Ho?

(Wok Ho is still oblivious to the question, as he admires Santa's new look!)

Santa   Mr *Ho*....Mr *Ho*....MR *HO*! Have you any sug....hang on! I've got it! Ho! Ho! Ho! That will be my catchphrase! What do you all think?

All   HO! HO! HO! PERFECT!

Song Ho! Ho! Ho! (tracks 7 & 33, lyrics p25)
(Santa's entourage, supported by the whole cast)

*(As the **intro music** then plays **(track 34)**, the whole cast gathers on and around the stage with the five hosts at the centre. Fade the music when all are in position.)*

If using our digital backdrops, select 'backdrop 1'

Scene 7

Rudolph   And today Santa is online! Modern technology means we can now track his journey round the world on Christmas Eve as he delivers our presents! That's Christmas brought bang up to date!

Festivius M.   So, everybody, that brings us almost to the end of our presentation about how Christmas came to be. It hasn't been too boring for you, we hope?

All   NO!

Gabriel   And you've all learned something you didn't know before?

All   YES!

Erika W.   And you've all had fun and been entertained?

All   YES!

Charles D.   Then our job here is done! As you leave us, we wish you everything that you wish for yourselves this festive season.

Gabriel   May peace, love and goodwill fill your homes and your hearts. And hey, don't forget to have fun too!

All   MERRY CHRISTMAS, ONE AND ALL!

If using our digital backdrops, select 'backdrop 8'

Song # Roll On Christmas Day

(tracks 8 & 35, lyrics p26)

(The whole cast)

THE END

A Time To Celebrate

Chorus   *A time to celebrate, a time for family,*
A time for presents and for hanging baubles on the tree.
A time for caring and for sharing,
A time for lots of ho-ho-ho!
That's the Christmas we have come to know.

Verse 1   But can you guess how it all started?
It hasn't always been about Santa on his sleigh!
And so we're gonna see the history
Of how we made our way
To the kind of Christmas we enjoy today,
And that is.....

Chorus   *A time to celebrate.....*

Verse 2   Now just sit back and let us show you
How things like turkey dinners and stockings came to be,
Why under mistletoe's the place to go
And why, traditionally,
We all gather for the ultimate party!
Because it's.....

Chorus   *A time to celebrate.....*

Saturnalia

Chorus *Oh, Saturnalia, Saturnalia,*
When people feast and act the clown
And everything is always topsy-turvy,
Back to front and upside down!

Verse 1 This celebrated ancient festival,
In December's darkest days,
Let the citizens of Rome make merry
In the strangest ways.
Masters became the slaves and slaves the masters,
A twist on social role,
And to eat and to drink 'til they all could eat
And drink no more was the goal!

Chorus *Oh, Saturnalia, Saturnalia.....*

Verse 2
(All) And if you'd been around you would have witnessed
Some quite confusing sights;
(Gladiators) Women wearing armour facing-off
In gladiator fights!
(The Wealthy) And wealthy people dressed in rags and giving
Their money to the poor!
(The Poor) Such a pity it lasted for one short week,
We could always do with some more!

Chorus *Oh, Saturnalia, Saturnalia.....*

Banish The Winter Blues

Verse 1

Bitter was the weather and dark were the days.
(dark the days, dark the days)
Harsh was the frozen ice and snow.
(ice and snow, ice and snow)
Wrapped in our furs by the fire's warming blaze,
(warming blaze, warming blaze)
We waited for winter to go.
(winter to go, winter to go, winter to go)

Chorus

Winter Solstice gives an excuse
To tap all our barrels of booze!
Twelve days of feasting means we cut loose
And banish the winter blues!

(shout loudly) *Skål!*

Verse 2

Sometimes we looked out but then what did we see?
(did we see, did we see)
Fields decked in white and skies of grey.
(skies of grey, skies of grey)
When would the sun end this bleak misery
(misery, misery)
And frosts, in its warmth, melt away?
(frosts melt away, frosts melt away, frosts melt away)

Chorus *Winter Solstice gives an excuse.....*

Verse 3

Grain supplies ran low, cattle had to be killed.
(to be killed, to be killed)
Fresh meat! An early taste of Yule!
(taste of Yule, taste of Yule)
Then will we feast 'til our bellies be filled.
(will be filled, will be filled)
The darkness shall no longer rule!
(no longer rule, no longer rule, no longer rule)

Chorus *Winter Solstice gives an excuse.....*

Repeat Chorus

Shout *Skål!*

Hallelujah!

Chorus   *Hallelujah! Hallelujah! Hallelujah!*
Jesus is born!
Hallelujah! Hallelujah! Hallelujah!
Jesus is born!

Verse 1   Welcome to Bethlehem, it's just a quiet little town.
But here in Bethlehem there's something big going down!
Well, in a stable beneath a star so bright
Something magical's happening tonight;
There in a manger a sleeping baby lies
As angels' heavenly voices fill the skies,
Singing.....

Chorus   *Hallelujah.....*

Verse 2   Yes, here in Bethlehem, God has delivered His son,
And so to Bethlehem shepherds and wise men have come.
They all give thanks for the new born baby king
Then lay before Him the presents that they bring.
And all are watching with wonder in their eyes,
As angels' heavenly voices fill the skies,
Singing.....

Chorus   *Hallelujah.....*

Repeat Chorus

No More Christmas

Verse 1

(Puritans/Soldiers) We don't believe in Christmas fun
Because it threatens piety!
We don't permit extravagance,
Or tolerate frivolity.
There won't be any festival –
You're not allowed to decorate.
We'll stick to Puritan beliefs
And punish those who celebrate!

Chorus

(Revellers)   *Can we party just a bit?*
(P/S)   *No you can't! Get over it!*
(Revellers)   *A teeny weeny sip of ale?*
(P/S)   *If you want to go to jail!*
(Revellers)   *How about a song and dance?*
(P/S)   *Are you kidding? Not a chance!*
And just so you understand.....
NO MORE CHRISTMAS!
IT'S BEEN BANNED!

Verse 2

(All)   Well, soldiers now patrol the streets
With one intent, their task is clear.
They will arrest the merry-makers,
Stamping out all Christmas cheer,
And seek out those preparing feasts
So they can take the food away,
While shops and business must stay open
Just like any other day.

Chorus   *Can we party just a bit.....*

Repeat Chorus

The Victorians

Verse 1 *(All)* Prince Albert married Victoria
And came to join us here.
He introduced new Christmas customs –
Such a bright idea!
A favourite feature he passed on
From life in Germany
Would add some glamour to your house;
The good old Christmas tree!

Chorus

(All) *The Victorians loved their Christmas.*
Yes, they really had a ball!
(Victorians) *Raise a glass – God save the Queen!*
And goodwill to one and all!
(All) *If you reckon they were stuffy,*
Prim and proper some might say,
Think about the things they started,
Things we all enjoy today!

Verse 2

(Victorian 1) Well, most important is family time,
With children centre-stage.
(Victorian 2) And choirs of Christmas carol singers
Now are all the rage!
(Victorian 3) The shops are full of gifts to buy
To place beneath our tree
(All) And greetings cards are mass-produced,
Hung up for all to see!

Chorus   *The Victorians loved their Christmas.....*

Verse 3 *(All)* A turkey dinner was popular
But mostly for the rich!
Mince pies were made but now with fruit,
A very modern switch!
The Christmas cracker had a surge
In popularity,
While Dickens stories told of peace
And love and charity.

Chorus   *The Victorians loved their Christmas.....*

Ho! Ho! Ho!

Chorus

He puts his red suit on, buckles-up his belt
And then he's ready to go, go, go!
His sleigh's fully-loaded as he hits the skies
With a twinkle in his eye and a...
'Ho! Ho! Ho!'

Verse 1

He's a fella who goes by many names,
And you're free to take your pick.
Father Christmas, Santa Claus and Papa Noël,
Kris Kringle or Saint Nick.
He's had some image changes
He's played around with style,
But now he's settled on a look
Which, in anybody's book,
Is bound to raise a smile!

Chorus

He puts his red suit on.....

Verse 2

He's a fella we hope will be calling in
For a sherry and mince pie.
If we're very well-behaved and we do as we're told,
Then maybe he'll drop by?
It's always been his mission,
Throughout the centuries,
To bring a little bit of joy
To every girl and boy,
And boy, how he succeeds!

Chorus

He puts his red suit on.....

Instrumental

(Santa leads a dance routine!)

Chorus

He puts his red suit on.....

Roll On Christmas Day

Verse 1
When you sit and think
About what Christmas will bring,
What might be the most important thing?
The gifts round the tree?
So many good things to eat?
Well, Christmas means a little more to me.
Oh oh.....

Verse 2
It's more than enough
To see a smile lighting up
All the faces of the ones you love.
And just being near
To everyone you hold dear,
Well, that's the wonder of this time of year.
And as the winter winds
Bring their icy chill,
We'll be wrapped up safe and warm
In a blanket of good will.

Chorus
Roll on Christmas Day,
We know good times are on their way,
Let your home be filled with joy and laughter.
Lift your voices high
And let your troubles pass you by,
And may peace be in your heart forever after.

Repeat Chorus
Roll on Christmas Day.....
(Oh oh.....)

STAGING AND PRODUCTION SUGGESTIONS

'How Christmas Came To Be' has been written to be adaptable to most school hall set-ups, whether you have a stage or not. Below is just one representation of a possible staging layout.

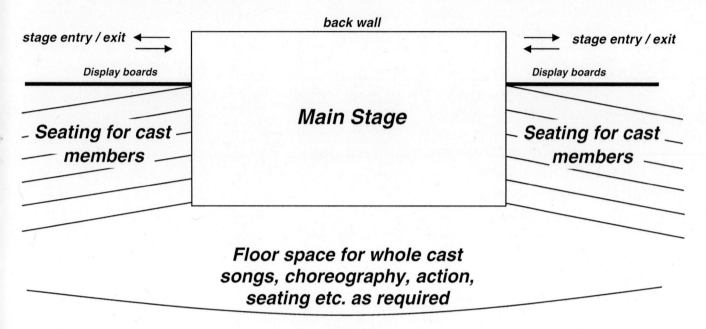

- *Scenery* – We recommend using our digital backdrops (see website for details – www.edgyproductions.com), but if not, decorate the back wall behind the stage, as well as the display boards behind the seated areas, with pictures of the iconic characters and scenes mentioned in the script. A large banner with the show's title could sit prominently above.

- *Furniture* – Not a lot required: a small stool for Senilius in scene 1, which can be used by Mary in scene 3, maybe a chaise if available for scene 5 and a rocking chair for Santa in scene 6.

- *Props (listed by scene)*
  Scene 1: A goblet. An ear trumpet (small cone of card covered in silver paper) wrapped up. A sword.
  Scene 2: A pile of twigs. A log. A sprig of mistletoe. A small wooden barrel.
  Scene 3: A doll. A manger. Three wise men's gifts. Toy sheep.
  Scene 4: A wrapped parcel. Two baskets of groceries. A pewter tankard.
  Scene 5: A small, green artificial Christmas tree. A box of tree decorations including an angel for the top. A dustpan and brush.
  Scene 6: A yellow Santa outfit on a hanger. A pink Santa outfit on a hanger.

- *Costume* – For individual character suggestions, **see page 29.**

- **_Use of Space_** – Large groups can be involved in the performance of most of the songs. A space on the floor in front of the main stage could be used to accommodate extra bodies. In this space, for some songs, the cast could perform dance routines. A seating area for resting performers could be allocated each side of the stage. This lets them enjoy the performance as part of the audience, allows easy movement on and off the stage, and of course eliminates the need for back-stage supervision.

- **_Audience seating_** – The audience could be in one block facing the stage, or in two blocks separated by an aisle wide enough for the entrance and exit of some characters to and from the back.

Of course, should you have any questions, or if you want further advice about putting on this musical, please email us and we'll be happy to give you all the information you need.

NB - a spoken line is defined as each time a character speaks, usually between 1 & 5 actual lines of text.

Speaking Character	Spoken Lines	Costume Suggestions
Rudolph	13	A red nose, a reindeer 'onesie' or brown top, leggings and antlers.
Gabriel	14	Traditional nativity angel costume, with wings and halo.
Charles Dickens	10	Victorian look – bow-tie, waistcoat and jacket. Long goatee beard.
Erika Winterbörn	9	Viking tunic and helmet. Fur shawl or wrap.
Festivius Maximus	10	Roman toga, laurel crown and red cloak.
Senilius	11	Roman toga and red cloak. White beard.
Tipsius	6	Plain brown or grey tunic.
Violentia	2	Armour breast plate over a white tunic. Greaves and a helmet.
Bratius	2	Plain brown or grey tunic.
Moodica	2	Plain brown or grey tunic.
Lavatoria	1	Long, belted purple dress, tiara and jewellery.
Olaf	6	Viking tunic and helmet. Fur shawl or wrap.
Astrid	5	Viking tunic and helmet. Fur shawl or wrap. Hair in plaits.
Cow 1	1	Cow 'onesie' or brown/black & white, leggings and a mask or horns.
Cow 2	1	Cow 'onesie' or brown/black & white, leggings and a mask or horns.
Cow 3	1	Cow 'onesie' or brown/black & white, leggings and a mask or horns.
Mary	1	Traditional nativity outfit
Joseph	1	Traditional nativity outfit
A Donkey	1	Donkey 'onesie' or grey top, leggings and a mask
An Angel	1	Traditional nativity outfit
A Shepherd	1	Traditional nativity outfit
A Wise Man	1	Traditional nativity outfit
Soldier 1	6	Cromwellian soldier – boots, tunic over wide/long collared shirt and helmet.
Soldier 2	5	Cromwellian soldier – boots, tunic over wide/long collared shirt and helmet.
Soldier 3	5	Cromwellian soldier – boots, tunic over wide/long collared shirt and helmet.
Reveller 1	2	Tunic and cloak (if man). Dress, pinafore and bonnet (if woman).
Reveller 2	2	Tunic and cloak (if man). Dress, pinafore and bonnet (if woman).
Reveller 3	1	Tunic and cloak (if man). Dress, pinafore and bonnet (if woman).
Reveller 4	1	Tunic and cloak (if man). Dress, pinafore and bonnet (if woman).
Prince Albert	7	Bow-tie, waistcoat, tailcoat and top hat. Bushy side-boards.
Child 1	2	Dress and bonnet (if girl). Knee-length stockings, shorts and jacket (if boy).
Child 2	2	Dress and bonnet (if girl). Knee-length stockings, shorts and jacket (if boy).
Child 3	2	Dress and bonnet (if girl). Knee-length stockings, shorts and jacket (if boy).
Queen Victoria	3	Black dress (padded-out), lace collar and her iconic headdress and crown.
Santa	5	Vest and pants to start, then traditional costume.
Mrs Santa	6	Grandmotherly floral dress and shawl.
Wok Ho	7	Think Gok Wan - sharp suit, black-rimmed glasses and a quiff.

A Time To Celebrate

Happy! ♩ = 134

Music & lyrics by Andrew Oxspring

‘How Christmas Came To Be’ by Andrew Oxspring & Ian Faraday

‘How Christmas Came To Be’ by Andrew Oxspring & Ian Faraday

Page 34

Saturnalia

Bright and very merry! ♩ = 90

Music & lyrics by Ian Faraday & Andrew Oxspring

Oh, Sa - tur - na - li - a, Sat - ur - na - li - a, when peo - ple feast and act the clown. And ev - ery- thing is al - ways top - sy - tur - vy, back to front and up - side

clown. And ev-ery-thing is al - ways top - sy - tur - vy,

back to front and up-side down!

Banish The Winter Blues

Slow, bleak ♩ = 81

Music & lyrics by Ian Faraday

V.1. Bit - ter was the wea - ther and dark were the days.
V.2. Some - times we looked out but then what did we see?
V.3. Grain sup - plies ran low, cat - tle had to be killed.

V.1. Dark the
V.2. Did we
V.3. To be

days, dark the days!
see, did we see!
killed, to be killed!

Ice and snow, ice and snow!
Skies of grey, skies of grey!
Taste of Yule, taste of Yule!

Harsh was the fro - zen ice and snow.
Fields decked in white and skies of grey.
Fresh meat! An ear - ly taste of Yule!

Wrapped in our furs by the
When would the sun end this
Then will we feast 'til our

 See p2

'How Christmas Came To Be' by Andrew Oxspring & Ian Faraday

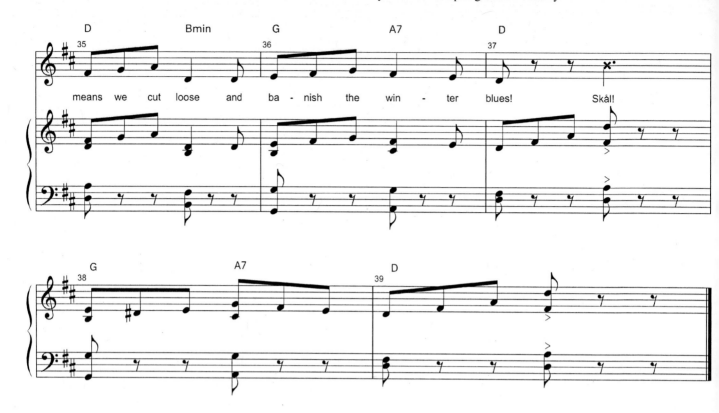

means we cut loose and ba - nish the win - ter blues! Skål!

Hallelujah!

With great joy! ♩ = 115

Music & lyrics by Andrew Oxspring

'How Christmas Came To Be' by Andrew Oxspring & Ian Faraday

'How Christmas Came To Be' by Andrew Oxspring & Ian Faraday

No More Christmas

To the point! ♩ = 180

Music & lyrics by Ian Faraday & Andrew Oxspring

V.1. (Puritans) We don't be-lieve in Christ-mas fun be-cause it threa-tens
V.2. (Revellers) Well sol-diers now pa-trol the streets with one in-tent - their

pi-e-ty! We don't per-mit ex-tra-va-gance or tol-er-ate fri-vol-i-ty. There
task is clear.... they will ar-rest the mer-ry-ma-kers, stam-ping out all Christ-mas cheer, and

won't be a-ny fes-ti-val - you're not al-lowed to dec-or-ate. We'll stick to Pur - i
seek out those pre-par-ing feasts so they can take the food a-way, while shops and bus-iness

tan be-liefs and pun-ish those who cel-e-brate!
must stay o-pen, just like a-ny o-ther day.

The Victorians

Music & lyrics by Ian Faraday

Chorus (All) The Vic-to-rians loved their Christ-mas. Yes, they real-ly had a ball! **(Victorians)** Raise a glass - God save the Queen! And good-will to one and all! **(All)** If you re-ckon they were stuf-fy, prim and pro-per some might say, think a-

bout the things they star - ted,   things we   all   en - joy   to - day!

Ho! Ho! Ho!

Very jolly! ♩ = 140

Music & lyrics by Andrew Oxspring

Chorus He puts his red suit on, buck - les up his belt and then he's rea - dy to go, go, go! His sleigh's ful - ly loa - ded as he hits the skies with a twin - kle in his eye and a.... Ho! Ho! Ho!

to next section after V.2. chorus

V.1. He's a
V.2. He's a

set - tled on a look which, in an - y - bo - dy's book, is bound to raise a smile!
lit - tle bit of joy t... o ev - ery girl and boy and boy, how he suc - ceeds!

rpt. 2 times %. next section
then cut to next section

Chorus He puts his Ho! Ho! Ho!

V.3. Instrumental

Chorus He puts his red suit on, buck-les up his belt and then he's rea-dy to go,

go, go! His sleigh's ful-ly loa-ded as he hits the skies with a twin-kle in his eye and a....

Ho! Ho! Ho!

Roll On, Christmas Day

Gently ♩ = 130

Music & lyrics by Andrew Oxspring

‘How Christmas Came To Be’ by Andrew Oxspring & Ian Faraday

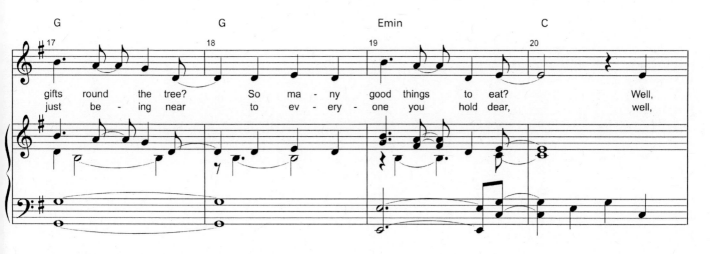

gifts round the tree? So ma - ny good things to eat? Well,
just be - ing near to ev - ery - one you hold dear, well,

to next section for rest of V.2.

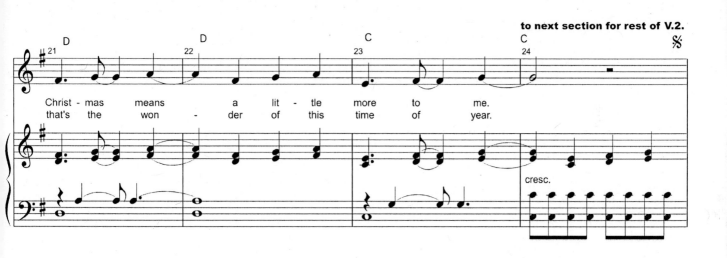

Christ - mas means a lit - tle more to me.
that's the won - der of this time of year.

cresc.

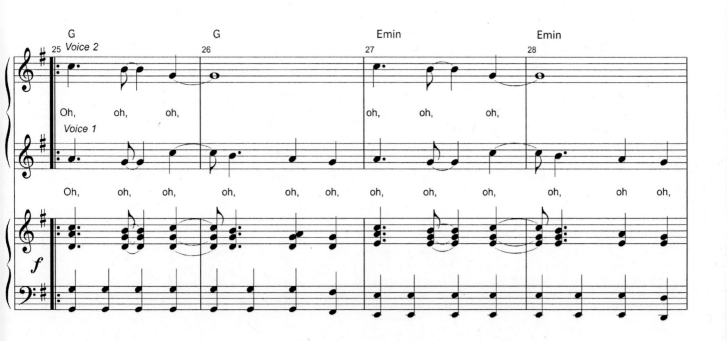

Voice 2
Oh, oh, oh, oh, oh, oh,

Voice 1
Oh, oh, oh, oh, oh, oh, oh, oh, oh, oh, oh oh,

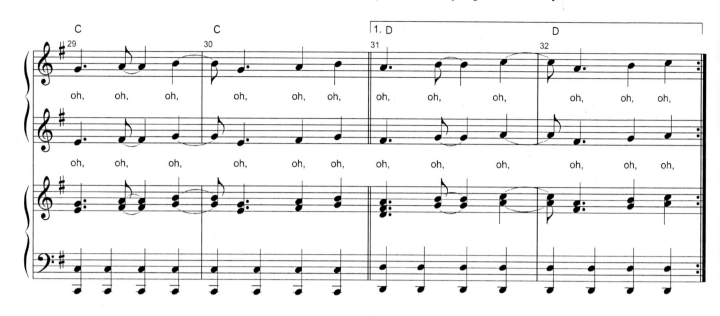

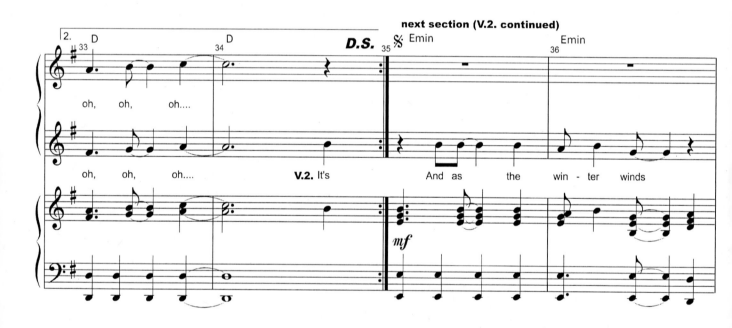

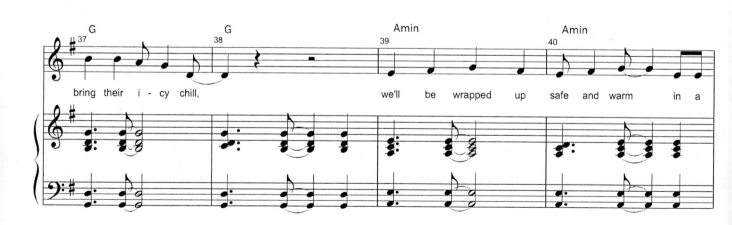

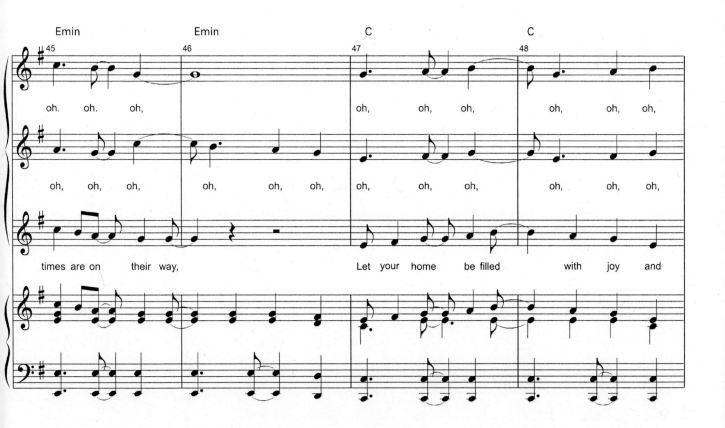

NOTES